Get the Wiggles Out

By JONATHAN PEALE

Illustrated by TOM HEARD

Music Arranged and Produced by
DREW TEMPERANTE

CANTATA
LEARNING

CANTATA
LEARNING

Published by Cantata Learning
1710 Roe Crest Drive
North Mankato, MN 56003
www.cantatalearning.com

A note to educators and librarians from the publisher: Cantata Learning has provided the following data to assist in book processing and suggested use of Cantata Learning product.

Publisher's Cataloging-in-Publication Data
Prepared by Librarian Consultant: Ann-Marie Begnaud
Library of Congress Control Number: 2015958182
    Get the Wiggles Out
    Series: School Time Songs
    Retold by Jonathan Peale
    Illustrated by Tom Heard
    Summary: A song that teaches students how to calm down at school by getting the wiggles out.
    ISBN: 978-1-63290-590-1 (library binding/CD)
    ISBN: 978-1-63290-573-4 (paperback/CD)
Suggested Dewey and Subject Headings:
    Dewey: E 395.5
    LCSH Subject Headings: Courtesy – Juvenile literature. | Students – Juvenile literature. | Courtesy – Songs and music – Texts. | Students – Songs and music – Texts. | Courtesy – Juvenile sound recordings. | Students – Juvenile sound recordings.
    Sears Subject Headings: Helping behavior. | Courtesy. | Students. | School songbooks. | Children's songs. | Popular music.
    BISAC Subject Headings: JUVENILE NONFICTION / School & Education. | JUVENILE NONFICTION / Music / Songbooks. | JUVENILE NONFICTION / Social Topics / Manners & Etiquette.

Book design and art direction, Tim Palin Creative
Editorial direction, Flat Sole Studio
Music direction, Elizabeth Draper
Music arranged and produced by Drew Temperante

Printed in the United States of America in North Mankato, Minnesota.
122016   0357CGF16R

ACCESS THE MUSIC!

SCAN CODE WITH MOBILE APP

CANTATALEARNING.COM

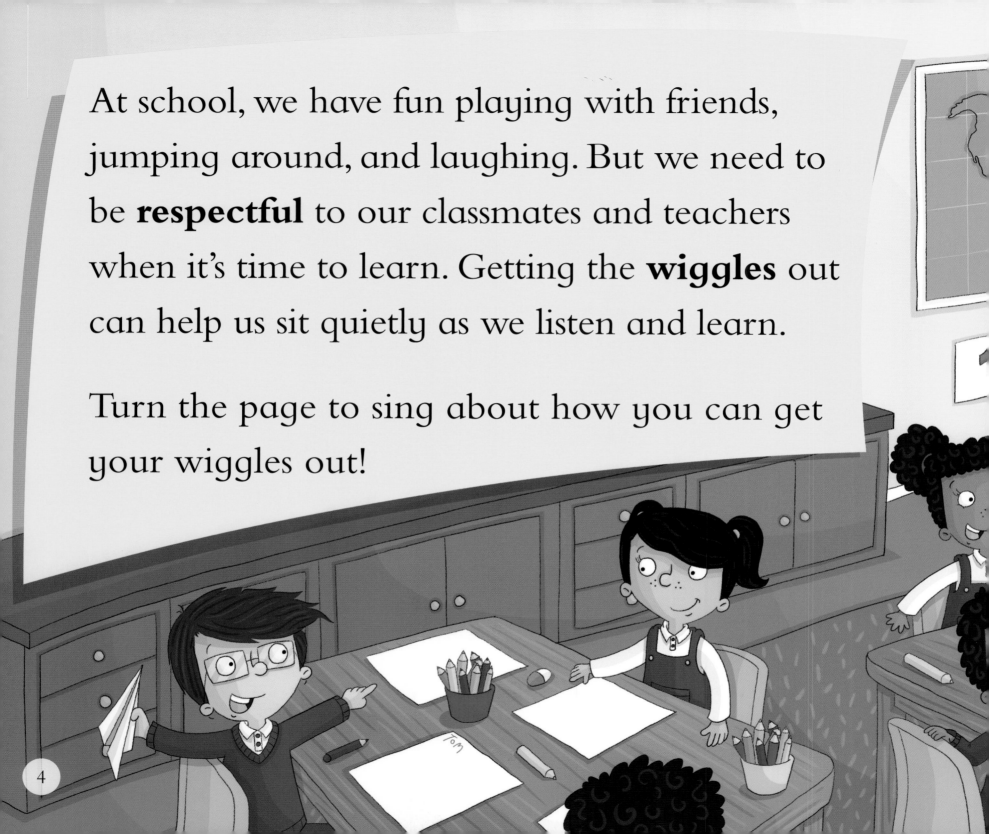

At school, we have fun playing with friends, jumping around, and laughing. But we need to be **respectful** to our classmates and teachers when it's time to learn. Getting the **wiggles** out can help us sit quietly as we listen and learn.

Turn the page to sing about how you can get your wiggles out!

We wiggle, wiggle, wiggle.
We wiggle all about.
Then we sit very still
when we get the wiggles out!

Wiggle up high.
Wiggle down low.
Wiggle with a hand.
Wiggle with a toe!

We wiggle, wiggle, wiggle.
We wiggle all about.
Then we sit very still
when we get the wiggles out!

Wiggle like a monkey
in a monkey tree.
Eat a sweet banana,
but save a bite for me!

We wiggle, wiggle, wiggle.
We wiggle all about.

Then we sit very still
when we get the wiggles out!

Wiggle with your friends.

Wiggle all alone.

Now stand like a tree.

Now sit like a stone.

We wiggle, wiggle, wiggle.

We wiggle all about.

Then we sit very still

when we get the wiggles out!

Wiggle like a worm
when you sit on the floor.
Wiggle side to side.
Then wiggle once more.

We wiggled out the wiggles.

There are no more wiggles in.

We wiggled out the wiggles,
and now we can begin!

We wiggled, wiggled, wiggled.
We wiggled all about.

Now we're sitting very still
because we got the wiggles out.

SONG LYRICS
Get the Wiggles Out

We wiggle, wiggle, wiggle.
We wiggle all about.
Then we sit very still
when we get the wiggles out!

Wiggle up high.
Wiggle down low.
Wiggle with a hand.
Wiggle with a toe!

We wiggle, wiggle, wiggle.
We wiggle all about.
Then we sit very still
when we get the wiggles out!

Wiggle like a monkey
in a monkey tree.
Eat a sweet banana,
but save a bite for me!

We wiggle, wiggle, wiggle.
We wiggle all about.

Then we sit very still
when we get the wiggles out!

Wiggle with your friends.
Wiggle all alone.
Now stand like a tree.
Now sit like a stone.

We wiggle, wiggle, wiggle.
We wiggle all about.

Then we sit very still
when we get the wiggles out!

Wiggle like a worm
when you sit on the floor.
Wiggle side to side.
Then wiggle once more.

We wiggled out the wiggles.
There are no more wiggles in.
We wiggled out the wiggles,
and now we can begin!

We wiggled, wiggled, wiggled.
We wiggled all about.

Now we're sitting very still
because we got the wiggles out.

Get the Wiggles Out

Hip Hop (Funk/Soul)
Drew Temperante

Chorus

We wig-gle, wig-gle, wig-gle. We wig-gle all a-bout. Then we sit ver-y still when we get the wig-gles out!

Verse

1. Wig-gle up high. Wig-gle down low. Wig-gle with a hand. Wig-gle with a toe!

Chorus

Verse 2
Wiggle like a monkey
in a monkey tree.
Eat a sweet banana,
but save a bite for me!

Chorus

Verse 3
Wiggle with your friends.
Wiggle all alone.
Now stand like a tree.
Now sit like a stone.

Chorus

Verse 4
Wiggle like a worm
when you sit on the floor.
Wiggle side to side.
Then wiggle once more.

Chorus
We wiggled out the wiggles.
There are no more wiggles in.
We wiggled out the wiggles,
and now we can begin!

Chorus
We wiggled, wiggled, wiggled.
We wiggled all about.
Now we're sitting very still
because we got the wiggles out.

GLOSSARY

respectful—treating someone with kindness, such as listening to your teacher while at school

wiggles—quick, twisting and turning movements

GUIDED READING ACTIVITIES

1. In this story, the children try to "get the wiggles out." What does it mean to have the wiggles?

2. There are times when it is okay to move about and times you should sit still and be quiet. When is it okay to move about? When should you sit still and be quiet?

3. What do you do to get the wiggles out? Do you run, or jump, or crawl? What helps you get ready to sit still and listen?

TO LEARN MORE

Laffin, Jenna. *How Do We Listen?* Minneapolis: Cantata Learning, 2016.

Manushkin, Fran. *Keep Dancing, Katie*. North Mankato, MN: Picture Window Books, a Capstone imprint, 2015.

Ponto, Joanna. *Being Respectful*. New York: Enslow Publishing, 2016.

Ziefert, Harriet. *Wiggle like an Octopus*. Maplewood, NJ: Blue Apple Books, 2011.